ENLIGHTENED PUBLICATIONS

Queensland, Australia.

www.enlightenedpublications.com

www.michaelvday.com

©Michael V. Day 2020

All Rights Reserved.

Photographic attribution abreviations

©BWC: Bahá'í World Centre
©USBNA: United States Bahá'í National Archives
©BIC: Bahá'í International Community
©BWNS: Bahá'í World News Service
©ANBA: Australian National Bahá'í Archives
©AWM: Australian War Memorial

Graphic design: William McGuire

Research associate: Fuad Izadinia

Editorial assistance: Marjorie Tidman; Keith McDonald

The Story of the Shrine of the Báb

The information in this photo book is drawn from a trilogy by Michael V. Day which tells the story of the Shrine of the Báb.

For the full story of the Shrine, with its pulsating dramas, heart-stopping moments, towering personalities, and inspiration, you are invited to read the trilogy (See covers on page 56):

1. **Journey to a Mountain** — The Story of the Shrine of the Báb — Volume I :1850-1921

2. **Coronation on Carmel** — The Story of the Shrine of the Báb — Volume II: 1922-1963

3. **Sacred Stairway** — The Story of the Shrine of the Báb — Volume III: 1963-2001

The trilogy is published by George Ronald Publisher: **www.grbooks.com**

Also available via Bahá'í Distribution Services, Bahá'í bookstores, and Amazon. **E-book editions available on Kindle.**
For detailed information visit: **www.michaelvday.com**

About the author

Michael V. Day is a newspaper journalist who lived and worked near the Shrine of the Báb when editor of the Bahá'í World News Service (2003-2006). Born and raised in New Zealand, he lives in Queensland, Australia, with his wife, Dr Chris Day.

Tributes

Journey to a Mountain

'An exhilarating read, a meticulously researched work...I was drawn in and needed to continue.' — Dr Janet A. Khan (Australia)

Coronation on Carmel

'Truly a masterpiece.' — Mr 'Alí Nakhjavaní (France)

Sacred Stairway

'Volume three was just as good as the first two, which were both excellent.' — Douglas Henck (USA)

With loving dedication to my wife, Dr Chris Day

And in fond memory of these other unwavering Bahá'í women:
Freda Butler, Emily Hughes, Beryl Osbahr, Linda Hight, Carol Corson, Judy Hassall.

Prayers by the Báb

"Is there any Remover of difficulties save God?
Say: Praised be God! He is God! All are His servants,
and all abide by His bidding!"

"O Lord! Unto Thee I repair for refuge, and toward all Thy signs I set my heart.

O Lord! Whether travelling or at home, and in my occupation or in my work,
I place my whole trust in Thee.

Grant me then Thy sufficing help so as to make me independent of all things,
O Thou Who art unsurpassed in Thy mercy!

Bestow upon me my portion, O Lord, as Thou pleasest, and cause me
to be satisfied with whatsoever Thou hast ordained for me.

Thine is the absolute authority to command."

Queen of Carmel

The Shrine of the Báb | A story in photographs 1850 – 2011

Michael V. Day

Quotations

He, verily, loveth the spot which hath been made the seat of His throne, which His footsteps have trodden, which hath been honoured by His presence, from which He raised His call, and upon which He shed His tears.

— Bahá'u'lláh (1817-1892)

From the bottom of the mountain to the Shrine there will be nine terraces, and nine more terraces will be built from the Shrine to the top of the mountain. Gardens with colourful flowers will be laid down on all these terraces.

— 'Abdu'l-Bahá (1844-1921)

This beautiful and majestic path which extends from the Shrine of the Báb to the City of Haifa in line with the greatest avenue in that blessed city… will subsequently be converted, as foreshadowed by the Centre of the Covenant, into the Highway of the Kings and Rulers of the World.

— Shoghi Effendi (1897-1957)

The beauty and magnificence of the Gardens and Terraces… are symbolic of the nature of the transformation which is destined to occur both within the hearts of the world's peoples and in the physical environment of the planet.

— The Universal House of Justice (International governing council of the Bahá'í Faith)

Tribute To The Shrine Of The Báb (extract)

High, immeasurably high, is this Shrine, the lofty, the most great, the most wondrous. Exalted, immeasurably exalted is this Resting-place, the fragrant, the pure, the luminous, the transcendent. Glorified, immeasurably glorified is this Spot, the most august, the most holy, the most blessed, the most sublime…

Blessed, immeasurably blessed is the one who visits thee and circles around thee, who serves at thy threshold, waters thy flowers, inhales the fragrance of holiness from thy roses, celebrates thy praise and magnifies thy station for the love of God, He who has created thee in this most hallowed and luminous, this most exalted, august and wondrous age.

— Shoghi Effendi (1897-1957)

People and Places

'Abdu'l-Bahá (1844–1921): Head of the Bahá'í Faith 1892–1921; eldest son of Bahá'u'lláh. Builder of original Shrine building. https://www.bahai.org/abdul-baha

Acre: English name for ancient walled city on north coast of Israel. In Hebrew "'Akko", in Arabic "'Akká".

Arcade: series of adjoining arches with columns which provide a walkway around the Shrine.

The Báb (1819–1850): Divine Messenger with an independent revelation. The forerunner of Bahá'u'lláh. He was born in Shiraz and executed in Tabriz. He is buried in a vault of the Shrine of the Báb. https://www.bahai.org/the-bab/life-the-bab

Bahá'í Faith: Independent world religion founded by Bahá'u'lláh. For more information, see: www.bahai.org

Bahá'í World Centre: The worldwide Bahá'í community's international administrative centre in Haifa.

Bahá'u'lláh (1817–1892): Divine Messenger. The Prophet-Founder of the Bahá'í Faith. He was born in Tehran and died at Bahjí, outside Acre. He directed that the Shrine of the Báb be built on Mount Carmel.

Fariborz Sahba (Born 1948): Persian-born architect of 19 garden terraces of the Shrine of the Báb.

Mount Carmel: Headland looking over the Bay of Haifa.

Persia: Country now known as Iran.

Shoghi Effendi (1897–1957): Head of the Bahá'í Faith from 1921–1957. Built the arcade and superstructure in accordance with the wishes of 'Abdu'l-Bahá, his grandfather.

Shrine of the Báb: Structure on Mount Carmel in Haifa where the sacred remains of the Báb are interred. Holiest place for Bahá'ís apart from the Shrine of Bahá'u'lláh. 'Abdu'l-Bahá is also interred there pending the construction of His own Shrine.

Superstructure: Structure built on top of the original stone mausoleum.

Terraces: The Shrine of the Báb sits on a Terrace (known informally as Terrace #10). There are 18 other garden terraces with #19 at the peak.

Universal House of Justice: The international governing council of the Baha'i Faith.

William Sutherland Maxwell (1874-1952): Canadian-born architect of the arcade and superstructure of the Shrine of the Báb. https://www.bahai.org/the-bab/shrine

Timeline

1850: Martyrdom of the Báb in Tabriz, Persia, the rescue of His sacred remains, their transfer to Tehran.

1891: Bahá'u'lláh points to the site for the future Shrine of the Báb on Mount Carmel in the Holy Land and directs 'Abdu'l-Bahá, His eldest son and successor, to build it, transfer the sacred remains from Persia and inter them.

1892: Bahá'u'lláh passes away.

1898: Those carrying the sacred remains of the Báb begin the journey from Persia to Acre (now 'Akko) in the Holy Land. The first Western pilgrims arrive.

1899: The casket containing the sacred remains of the Bab arrives in Acre.
Construction of the Shrine of the Báb begins with the laying of its foundation stone.

1909: Interment by 'Abdu'l-Bahá of the sacred remains of the Báb in a vault in the Shrine of the Báb.

1921: 'Abdu'l-Bahá passes away and is interred in a vault in the Shrine of the Báb.

1922: Shoghi Effendi, the new head of the Faith, begins the work of extending the gardens, terraces and the Shrine itself.

1944: Shoghi Effendi unveils the model of the arcade and domed superstructure of the Shrine of the Báb.

1948: The project to build the arcade and superstructure begins, as marble and granite is obtained and carved in Italy, and shipped to Haifa.

1953: The project completed, a golden dome shines over Haifa.

1957: Shoghi Effendi passes away and is laid to rest in London.

1963: The newly elected international governing council of the Bahá'í Faith, the Universal House of Justice, takes on the responsibility for the Shrine of the Báb.

1987: The Universal House of Justice appoints Mr Fariborz Sahba, the architect of the Bahá'í House of Worship in India (the "Lotus Temple"), to design and project manage the construction of the Terraces of the Shrine of the Báb.

1990: Work begins on the project to build the 19 Terraces of the Shrine of the Báb.

2001: The inauguration of the Terraces of the Shrine of the Báb.

2005: A project to restore and refurbish the Shrine of the Báb begins.

2008: The Shrine of the Báb is one of the Bahá'í sites inscribed on the UNESCO World Heritage List.

2011: The shining new tiles of the dome of the Shrine of the Báb are unveiled at the completion of the restoration project.

An Illustrated Guide

This book is an illustrated guide to events that led to today's spectacular vision of the Shrine of the Báb and its garden terraces on Mount Carmel in Haifa, Israel. For members of the Bahá'í Faith around the world, the Shrine is a site of pilgrimage, the holiest place in the world apart from the Shrine of Bahá'u'lláh across the bay. It is inscribed on the World Heritage List as part of the cultural heritage of humanity. The Shrine is the mausoleum of the prophetic figure known as the Báb.

The Báb

The Báb (1819-1850), arose with a divine message in Persia (modern Iran) in 1844. The Báb quickly attracted large numbers of followers throughout the country. His fame soon spread into Europe, Asia and beyond. The Báb, whose name means "The Gate", announced that He was the Forerunner and Herald of One who would bring a great message to humanity. That messenger was to be Bahá'u'lláh (1817-1892), the Prophet-Founder of the Bahá'í Faith, who declared His mission in 1863. His message was of the oneness of God, the oneness of humanity, and the essential oneness of the world's religions.

The Báb had a charismatic spiritual personality and an eloquent and melodious voice. His appearance was one of refinement in both clothing and physical features. The prayers He revealed continue to be recited today by Bahá'ís privately and at devotional meetings. During the 1840s, fanatical clergy became alarmed at the rapid growth of His following. They persuaded the authorities to instigate widespread persecutions. They wanted the execution of the Báb, which was ordered by the Prime Minister.

The martyrdom of the Báb took place in a barracks square (photograph opposite) in Tabriz on 9 July, 1850. This photograph was taken in later years.

A Hidden Treasure

In a daring night-time mission, the followers of the Báb recovered His sacred remains, which were intertwined with those of Anis, a loyal companion who was martyred with Him. The Báb's followers wrapped the precious remains in a shroud and placed them in a wooden coffin, which they concealed amidst bales of silk. A trusted band of men later took the coffin from Tabriz to Tehran where it was hidden in various places for nearly 50 years.

In 1868, Bahá'u'lláh, the Prophet-Founder of the Bahá'í Faith, arrived in the Holy Land, after 15 years as an exile in Baghdad and Adrianople (modern Edirne). In 1891 on Mount Carmel in Haifa, Bahá'u'lláh instructed His eldest son, 'Abdu'l-Bahá, to arrange the transfer of the remains of the Báb from Persia to the Holy Land when the time was right. He pointed to a nearby site and directed 'Abdu'l-Bahá to purchase it, and to inter the sacred remains of the Báb in a shrine which He should build there.

Running Throne

Bahá'u'lláh passed away in 1892. Under His Will, 'Abdu'l-Bahá became head of the Faith. Six years later, 'Abdu'l-Bahá commanded that the casket containing the sacred remains of the Báb be brought to the Holy Land. At His direction, those entrusted with this mission travelled on foot carrying the casket in a "running throne", a palanquin. This method of transporting sacred objects was similar to the way the Jews carried the "Ark of the Covenant". The casket went by running throne within Persia and then to Bagdad and via Damascus to Beirut. It travelled by sea from Beirut to Acre in January 1899.

Illustration of "Ark of the Covenant", which was transported as a running throne

'Abdu'l-Bahá concealed the casket until in 1909 He interred it in a vault in the Shrine He had built on the site chosen by Bahá'u'lláh.

Mirzá Asádu'lláh-i-Isfáhání (above), was appointed by 'Abdu'l-Bahá as the leader of those carrying the casket from Persia to the Holy Land.

Mirzá Asádu'lláh Khán (above, right), concealed the Báb's casket in Isfahan (1898) and helped with arrangements to take it out of Persia.

Muhammad Mustafá Bagdádí of Beirut (right), was involved in the protection and transfer of the casket of the Báb.

Houses of the German Templer colony lined the avenue leading from the sea to the base of Mount Carmel in Haifa (Engraving by J. Schumacher, 1877).

Halfway up the slope of Mount Carmel, a circle of cypress trees (right) indicates the spot where Bahá'u'lláh stood in 1891, when He pointed to the site for the Shrine of the Báb. Photograph taken in later years.

Builder of the Shrine

'Abdu'l-Bahá (1844-1921) was the head of the Bahá'í Faith from 1892 until 1921.

He began building the Shrine of the Báb in 1899. In 1909 He interred the Báb's casket in an underground vault of that mausoleum.

In 1921, 'Abdu'l-Bahá passed away. The casket containing His sacred remains was interred under the central northern room of the Shrine of the Báb.

In 2019, the Universal House of Justice announced that work on architectural plans was advancing for a Shrine for 'Abdu'l-Bahá.

For about one year from 1899 to 1900 'Abdu'l-Bahá hid the casket of the sacred remains of the Báb in the room of His beloved sister, Bahíyyih Khánum (1846-1932) (left), in the Acre house they both lived in (below, left).

'Abdu'l-Bahá moved the casket to Haifa, where He concealed it in a house in the area circled (below, right).

The inset of this photograph of Mount Carmel (above), probably taken in early 1900, shows a close-up view of the foundations of the Shrine and, behind them, the circle of cypress trees where some nine years earlier Bahá'u'lláh had pointed to the site for the Shrine.

Above and behind US Bahá'í pilgrim Edward Getsinger (left), is the construction site of the Shrine, probably in 1900, where considerable progress has been made.

A rudimentary stairway leads to the Shrine under construction (right). Photograph by Edward Getsinger, circa 1900.

Bahá'ís of Burma (Myanmar) in May 1898 (below), with the marble sarcophagus built for the Báb's sacred remains. It arrived in Haifa in 1899.

'Abdu'l-Bahá, at front in centre, with some Bahá'ís on the eastern side of the Shrine, circa 1914 (above, left). Shoghi Effendi, wearing a white scarf, is behind the grey-bearded elderly man to the left of 'Abdu'l-Bahá.

The Shrine of the Báb close to the time of interment of the sacred remains in 1909 (above, right).

A water tank above the reservoir just northwest of the Shrine (left).

The casket of 'Abdu'l-Bahá (right) leaves for His funeral service at the Shrine of the Báb in 1921 (below, left). The British High Commissioner, Sir Herbert Samuel (below), attended. Thousands thronged the entire route.

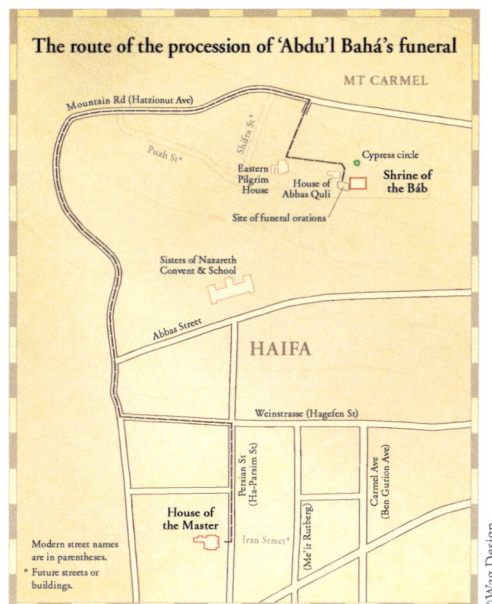

Shoghi Effendi (1897-1957), the eldest grandson of 'Abdu'l-Bahá, in his late teens. After he became head of the Faith in 1921, he quickly began developing the Shrine's terraces and extending its gardens as seen in these photos, taken in 1924.

A parade of lights illuminated the terraces down to Abbas Street in the mid-1930s (right). A light also shines from the roof of the Shrine of the Báb. To the left, 'Abdu'l-Bahá's room with its white walls and sloping room is on the roof of the house of 'Abbás-Qulí. At the far left, a light glows in the central room of the Pilgrim House. The top terrace is not yet extended far to the east. Boulders remain on the lower slope of Mount Carmel. The photographer was probably Effie Baker.

The terraces below the Shrine take shape in the 1930s (below). Photograph by Effie Baker.

The eastern side of the Shrine with the additional three rooms at the rear, which were completed in 1930. At left is the western wall of the custodian's house (demolished in the 1930s).

This bridge over Abbas Street, built in the 1930s, allowed the path through the terraces to continue down the mountain.

Properties adjacent to the edge of the terraces were acquired to allow for expansion.

The Maxwell family (left to right): The architect of the arcade and superstructure of the Shrine of the Báb, William Sutherland Maxwell (1974-1952). Mary Maxwell (1910-2000) in her teenage years. May Maxwell (1870-1940), prominent Bahá'í and wife of the architect, with their daughter Mary, who became the wife of Shoghi Effendi in 1937.

This beautiful colour rendition of the proposed design of the arcade and superstructure was drawn and painted by William Sutherland Maxwell.

The model made by William Sutherland Maxwell in 1944 of his design for the arcade and superstructure of the Shrine of the Báb (right).

A delicately beautiful depiction by Mr Maxwell of the proposed entrance and terraces of the Shrine (below).

The marble and granite for the arcade and superstructure were sourced and carved in Italy, and then transported by sea to Haifa beginning in November 1948. The sections were assembled on site.

Various photos of the colonnade and balustrade of the Shrine taking shape.

A shaft of light illuminates the construction site (right).

A key figure in the project to build the arcade and superstructure was Dr Ugo Giachery of Italy, pictured in later years with his wife, Angeline (below), who also contributed to the work.

Some Haifa residents thought the Shrine complete in 1950 when the arcade and balustrade were built (right) and then in April 1952 when the octagon was in place (below, left) but by May the same year it become clear that more was to come as work began on the drum, which would support the golden dome (below, right).

This glorious sight in April 1952 when the octagon and pinnacles were complete was just a prelude of things to come.

A family heads from the Pilgrim House towards the Shrine before the construction of the dome (opposite).

In 1953 the stonemason who built the dome, Abu Khalil (below), fixes into place one of the tiles.

Abu Khalil stands at the left of a colleague and the project manager Leroy Ioas (centre), who is also partially reflected in the gleaming tiles (far right).

Scaffolding still embraces the drum after the completion of the dome in 1953. Prominent Bahá'ís Amelia Collins (second from right) and Sylvia Ioas (right) stand with two friends near the bell before it was hoisted to the top of the dome.

Shoghi Effendi (1897-1957), who directed the construction of the arcade and superstructure of the Shrine of the Báb, pictured here just after completion (right). Shoghi Effendi called the Shrine "the Queen of Carmel".

Aerial view of the completed Shrine and its environs in 1953 (opposite).

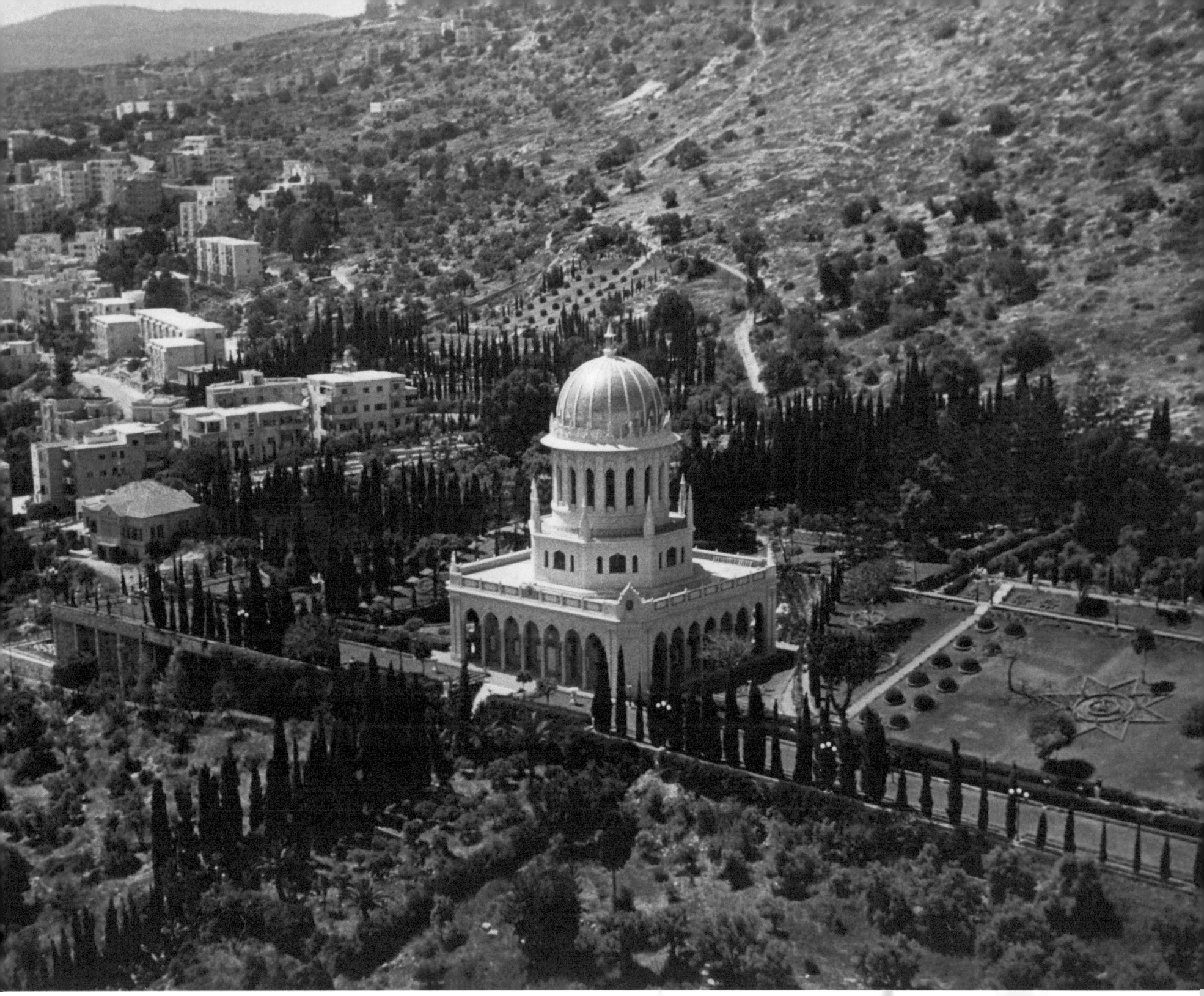

A postcard image not long after the completion of the dome shows the pathway up to the Shrine, as well as the area that almost half a century later would be the entrance plaza. The photo of the pathway down (right) also shows the tree-lined road below, now called Ben Gurion Avenue.

"Crowned in gold." One of the few colour photographs of the Shrine taken immediately after its completion in 1953.

Pictured in later years, the widow of Shoghi Effendi, Madame Ruhiyyih Rabbani (1910-2000), carried out a close-up inspection (left) of the tiles of the dome, (right, just after its completion). Bahá'ís knew her as 'Amatu'l-Bahá Rúhíyyih Khánum'. She assisted Shoghi Effendi in the project to complete the Shrine.

A 1956 Bahá'í publication included this photograph of the Shrine of the Báb (opposite).

Architect of the Terraces of the Shrine of the Báb, Mr Fariborz Sahba (above), shows a model of the project to Israeli statesman Mr Shimon Peres, who was foreign minister at the time.

Mr Hossein Amanat, architect of the administrative buildings to the east of the Terraces, with a model of the project (right). They were built at the same time as the Terraces and were completed in 2000 (above, right).

In 2001 Bahá'ís from around the world gathered in celebration of the inauguration of the Terraces of the Shrine of the Báb.

Mr Fariborz Sahba, architect of the Terraces of the Shrine of the Báb and project manager of their construction.

An early computer-generated model of the design of the Terraces (below).

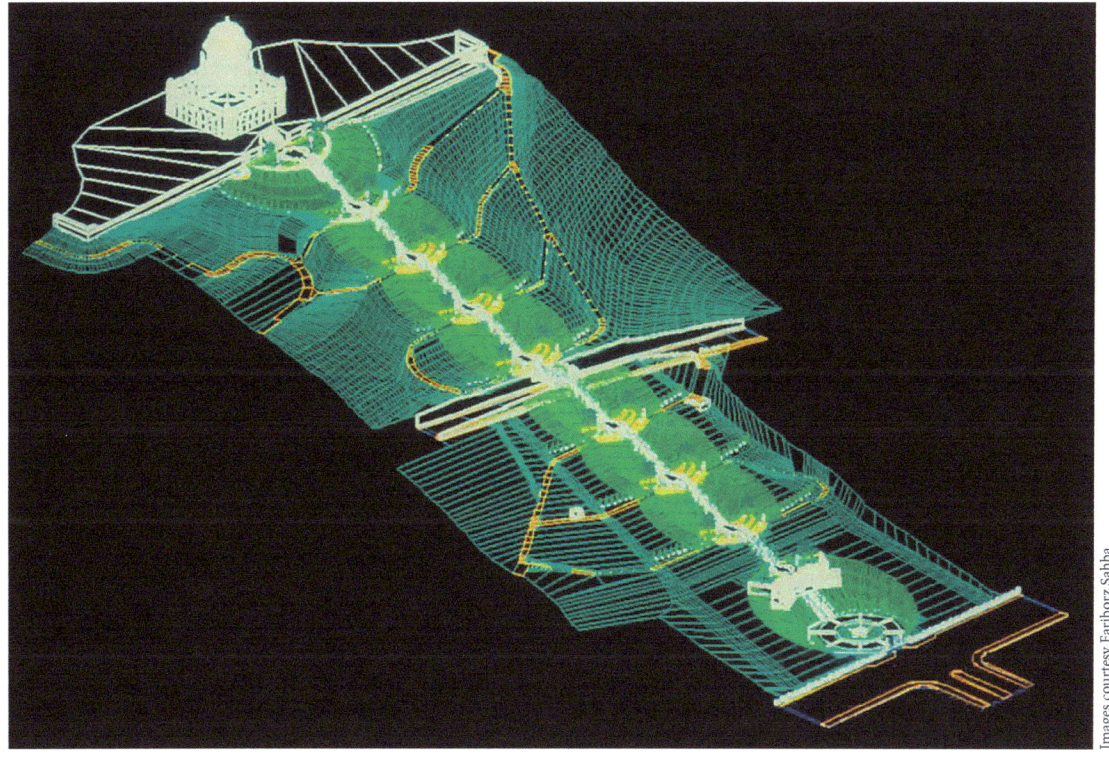

Models and sculpture from the design of the Terraces in 1988.

The site on Mount Carmel was cleared of rubble and vegetation at the start of the project (opposite), to build the garden Terraces.

Images courtesy Fariborz Sahba

The curves of the Terraces appeared in 1991. The project had begun in 1990 with the extension and strengthening of the central Terrace on which sits the Shrine of the Báb.

The bridge over Abbas Street as well as the Terraces begin to take shape.

The evening of the inauguration of the Terraces in May 2001 and the ascent the next day were events of great rejoicing by Bahá'ís around the world.

The fountain in the entrance plaza of the stairway to the Shrine of the Báb (opposite page).

A fountain on one of the completed Terraces (below) which embellish the Shrine of the Báb (right).

An aerial view of the Upper Terraces and some of the Lower Terraces, with the jewel-like Shrine of the Báb in the middle (opposite page). A seat and pool with potted plants are examples of exquisite details on the Terraces.

At night, the illuminated Shrine of the Báb and its stairway make a spectacular sight from the avenue below.

A pathway of light leading to the Shrine of the Báb (opposite).

The tiles of the dome lost their lustre over the decades. A cover was placed over the dome and its supporting structures during the 2005–2011 program of restoration and refurbishment of the whole building. New golden tiles replaced the originals.

Professionals and volunteers worked on the restoration project, which was completed in 2011.

The unveiling in April 2011 of the restored dome of the Shrine of the Báb revealed a shining spectacle.

Gilding and other processes restored the beauty of the Shrine of the Báb.

"The Queen of Carmel". The golden dome of the Shrine of the Báb shines resplendent.

Want to know more?

Want to read the exciting story with all its twists, turns, and triumphs? You can read it in: **Journey to a Mountain** - The Story of the Shrine of the Báb Volume I: 1850-1921 / **Coronation on Carmel** - Volume II: 1922-1963 / **Sacred Stairway** - Volume III: 1963-2001. To obtain copies visit: **www.grbooks.com**

Also available via Bahá'í Distribution Services, Bahá'í bookstores, and Amazon. **E-book editions available on Kindle**. For detailed information visit: **www.michaelvday.com**

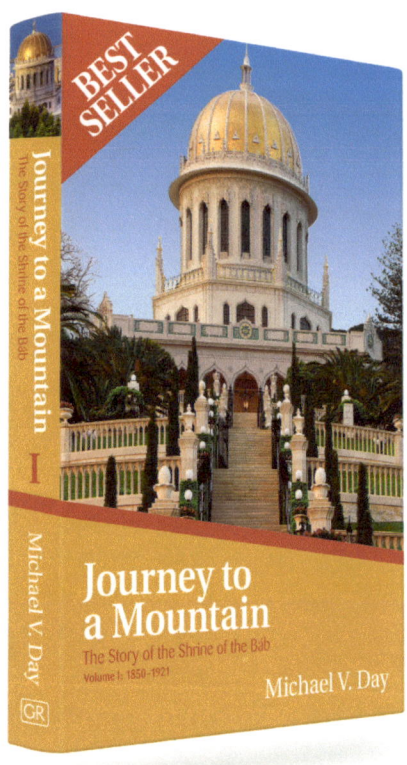

ISBN 978-0-85398-603-4

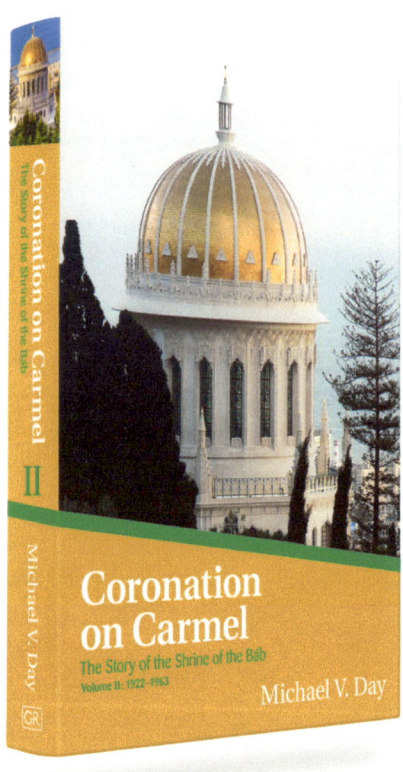

ISBN 978-0-85398-610-2

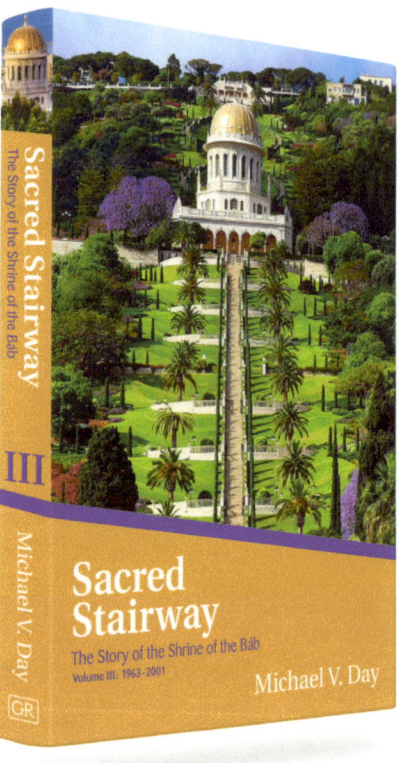

ISBN 978-0-85398-622-5

Back cover: The original Shrine of the Báb built by 'Abdu'l-Bahá was completed in the first decade of the 20th century.

www.ingramcontent.com/pod-product-compliance
Lightning Source LLC
Chambersburg PA
CBHW040936020526

44107CB00072B/1577